Keynotes to a Journey of Great Adventure

Diana Labrada

authorHOUSE®

AuthorHouse™
1663 Liberty Drive
Bloomington, IN 47403
www.authorhouse.com
Phone: 833-262-8899

This book is a work of non-fiction. Unless otherwise noted, the author and the publisher
make no explicit guarantees as to the accuracy of the information contained in this book
and in some cases, names of people and places have been altered to protect their privacy.

Published by AuthorHouse 05/26/2021

ISBN: 978-1-6655-2740-8 (sc)
ISBN: 978-1-6655-2739-2 (e)

Library of Congress Control Number: 2021910904

Print information available on the last page.

Any people depicted in stock imagery provided by Getty Images are models,
and such images are being used for illustrative purposes only.
Certain stock imagery © Getty Images.

This book is printed on acid-free paper.

King James Version (KJV)

Holy Bible, New International Version®, NIV® Copyright ©1973, 1978, 1984,
2011 by Biblica, Inc.® Used by permission. All rights reserved worldwide.

Scripture taken from the New King James Version®. Copyright © 1982
by Thomas Nelson. Used by permission. All rights reserved.

Common English Bible (CEB)

CONTENTS

DEDICATION

This book is dedicated especially to my stepfather, Jose C. Cano, for the great sacrifice; to my Pearl, my mother, Fernanda L. Cano, for her unconditional love; and to my bookmarks and reason for living—Juan, Jacklyn, Fred, Naomi, Zoe, Daizito, and Chris. Jesus E. Melhem Kuri- It is a great honor to have you as my father.

A special thank you to all my six sisters: Dalila Labrada Hinojosa, Veronica Neeley, Claudia Cano, Cecilia Cano, Cynthia Cano, Amelia Cano, and my two brothers, Fernando Labrada (my side kick) and Jose C. Cano Jr. (my baby brother). I love all of you guys.

A shout out to Rigo Moreno for your love and support, and to Linda Mahoney for all your help and dedication.

A special acknowledgment to Patty Avila, Ana Laura Muro, Adelaida Calvillo, and Rosie Cuellar, my angels on earth; Lydia Flores, my counselor and advisor; Rebecca Reyes for her special seed; Pam Tamez, Roberta Reyes and Marisa Olivares for their moral support; the members of my Fun Seekers club—Mari Lu, Tony, Cindy, Karina, Leroy—and to my faithful clients, friends, and followers.

To anyone who ever wronged me, I clearly remember neutralizing the situation, and loved you anyway.

My Dear Audience

I declare powerful, explosive chemical reactions to dissolve *all* harm prophesied, wished, testified, confessed, spoken, or even thought about you or your entire blood line in the name of Jesus. May your good deeds be richly multiplied. Arm yourself with knowledge of spiritual law, and you will find fulfillment in your journey to a great adventure—life. Bless and be blessed; whatever situation you may be going through, know that this too has been paid for in full!

Enlightened by His existence,

Love, Diana

THE JOURNEY

It is my hope that my keynotes will serve you well. If you learn anything from my collection of teachings and suggestions, let it be to trust in His plan.

Put an end to the struggle with a positive mindset and, in turn, allow healing. Remember that life is a ceremony, and you must celebrate and embrace it. Even if you fall ill, and death is inevitable, live life to the fullest.

Celebrate each moment and get to the finish line with pride. Keep in mind that your body has the ability to heal itself and is only "sound" as a whole—body, mind, and spirit.

Carrying heavy burdens through your entire journey will cause you to miss out on your season of laughter and dance, and ultimately your destiny. This life is not forever, so why wait until the end is near?

Lift any thoughts of limitations from yourself and trust in His promises. Don't put limitations on what God can do. The journey can be easier if you live with expectations, excitement, and enthusiasm.

DISCLAIMER

All of my keynotes are a personal story. I shared what has worked for me and the many clients I have treated. Everyone is different and results may vary. Suggestions are in no way intended to offend, defame or go against anyone's opinion, or to treat or diagnose illness. Please seek medical attention if you are ill. Hope to be your blessing.

MAKE PEACE WITH THE EARTH YOU WERE GIVEN DOMINION OVER

If you remember, in the book of Genesis, God gave us dominion over the earth and blessed us to be fruitful and multiply and replenish the earth and subdue it (Genesis 1:28). We have made a mess of all of this! People usually confess that God is in control. If God were in control, our world would not be in such danger. Human-made environmental damage would not be destroying our natural ecosystems. The list of our lack of responsibility is endless.

It is no wonder that my treatment room is always full of people suffering from depression, anxiety, unexplained mental instabilities, inflammation, or poor immunity. Modern-day lifestyle forces us to be in a hurry, working all day imprisoned by four walls while we wear well-insulated rubber shoes. This separates humans from direct physical contact with the vast supply of electrons on the surface of the earth, the fresh air, and the sunshine. Many scientific studies suggest that this disconnect is a major contributor to our physiological dysfunction and physical malady. I agree.

I teach my students and clients the importance of "earthing"—or grounding—themselves, which has been proven to improve sleep and reduce pain. Actually, once you get in the habit of grounding, it becomes fun and ceremonial, and you get to enjoy great healing benefits. I must admit that as a healthcare professional I was quite skeptical about the true effects of grounding, however after I experienced it for myself and saw the significant change in my health, I became a true believer, and felt in my heart that I should share my experience with the world with the intent to assist others to wellness.

Our air and water are compromised by toxic chemicals. It is an established fact that electrons from antioxidant molecules neutralize the reactive oxygen species, and free radicals involved in the body's inflammatory and over-all immune response; however, this topic is not always appreciated or even talked about.

Another great problem I've identified in my personal struggle for optimal health is that I can spend all day indoors imprisoned by four walls, with no fresh air, and walking on cement floors wearing insulated shoes, and I do not realize the damage I am incurring. My body is deprived of air, sun, the ground, and all that was meant for its repair and regeneration day to day.

Let's take a look at how our ancestors throughout history lived and walked. They spent their days very actively—hunting, fishing, gathering food and raw materials, and doing other strenuous duties. Most of them wore footwear made of very thin animal skin or plant material or they simply walked barefoot. They very often slept on the bare ground or covered the surface of the ground with animal skins or plant material. This gave them direct contact with electrons in the earth. The ground's abundant free electrons are electrically conductive. This mechanism enables the body to balance with electrical potential from the earth. So, if we chose to sleep on the ground, use animal skins or a mat, or walk barefoot, we could possibly stabilize the electrical environment of our cells, tissues, and organs as a whole. We live in a very fast-paced modern world that has separated our human race from the primordial flow of electrons found in the ground; for example, our streets and sidewalks are all paved with cement, our shoes are well-insulated, and our beds are cushioned by pillow-top mattresses.

It is no surprise that, in recent decades, there has been a great increase in documented cases of cancer, chronic illness, immune disorders, mental instability, anxiety, depression, and inflammatory diseases. Researchers have identified the causes as environmental factors. However, for whatever reason, human disconnection with the earth's surface is a topic that has been neglected, and not yet been addressed.

Most of the subjects I treat who perform grounding exercises and meditation describe symptomatic improvement, while most of the subjects who simply take medication do not.

Plain and simple—our bodies were not created to adapt to such high levels of speed (we are in such a hurry to do not a thing), which results in our brains releasing inflammation-causing hormones to keep up with the demand. The evidence of this is high levels of cortisol and other acids that are making us sick.

For more valuable information on grounding topics and health you may visit: Journal of Inflammation Research 2015. You may also be interested in the research on earthing effects by Dr Karol, Pawel Sokal in Poland and Clint Ober in USA. Also, Dr. Deepak Chopra, Endocrinologist, Author, expresses publicly in several educational videos found on the web on his personal positive experience and opinion on grounding.

I share with you the grounding tips that have worked for me:

1. I have dug a shallow hole in my backyard. It is deep enough for me to sit in. There I can chill, meditate, and relax barefoot. I call it "the meditation hole."

2. I embrace gardening, and I hug trees often.

3. Upon any sign of nervousness or anxiety, I run for the outdoors and I put all my senses to work:

A. Vision: I usually find a pretty tree, flowers in bloom, or if I'm lucky, a humming bird to admire.

B. Smell: I breathe in the air deeply and enjoy the aroma of fruit trees, peppermint, lemongrass, and other medicinal herbs I keep in my garden.

C. Taste: I usually go for a basil or peppermint leaf to chew on.

D. Hearing: I listen to birds sing or even cars passing by.

E. Touch: I grab a branch or play with dry leaves.

4. I embrace the hot sun God gave us. It provides vitamin D for my skin to absorb and strengthens my immune system, and it warms my bones. I sunbathe every chance I get.

5. I love the moon—the night light God left for me. I love moon bathing. I have found that it helps my eyesight, regulates my menstrual cycle, and lowers my blood pressure. Many Ayurveda experts believe moonlight triggers the release of melatonin, a hormone that our brain produces in response to darkness which promotes relaxation and sleep.

6. I breathe deeply and dance. In ancient times, we were forced to take shallow breaths. This was a skill that would enhance our hearing while we were out hunting so we could dominate our prey.

Here is a special reminder to you on the importance of breathing adequately. You are no longer hunting. Our cells need oxygen. Breathe deeply. Let your spine dance to the rhythm of life's breath.

Note: Grounding and meditation has worked for me and many of the clients I treat. Check with your Doctor before attempting any alternative preventive care especially if you are on prescribed medication. My keynotes are in no way intended to treat, diagnose disease or go against any medical advise.

WHEN DESTINY CHANGES YOUR VOCATION-STAND STILL IT MAY BE GOD REROUTING HIS WILL IN YOUR LIFE

High school graduation year 1989 was so exciting. Finally, I could choose my college of choice and become a doctor. Baylor College of Medicine, here I come!

The counselor at school worked hard to have my application ready for review and completion by my parents. Transcripts were printed, grades all in order—all that was needed was to complete the application process and schedule a tour to my school of choice.

On application day, the choices were simple: I wanted to be a medical doctor. The only way to get there was with full determination, top grades, and my parents' signatures. There were several colleges to choose from—St. Mary's University, University of the Incarnate Word, University of Texas—Pan American, and Baylor College of Medicine. I decided to stay home and complete all my basics at Pan-Am and then transfer to my dream college—Baylor College of Medicine.

The bell rang at three o'clock, and I was so eager to go home and present my vision to my parents. I was so nervous that my palms were sweating. In my excitement, I felt frantic. As soon as I was off the bus, I presented my applications to my mother, but at that time Dad was the head of household and made all the financial decisions. So she asked me to wait for him. My mother's English was limited too, so it was hard for her to complete applications.

At last, Dad was home. I proudly presented my applications to him; he was very proud of my grades and determination. However, he asked me in a serious tone, "And who is going to pay for this? I sure can't afford this." I bowed my head with sadness. My dreams, my vocation, and my choice now had to be second best. My dream to become a medical doctor was crushed. My parents could not afford to send me to medical school.

We are a family of nine children plus Mom and Dad. I made a decision in my heart to try to understand. Counselors at school were not the way they are nowadays. I guess the resources we have now were not available back in the day. Now I think back and say, "So why didn't my counselors explain I could have applied for student loans?"

For years, I struggled to find peace in my heart after settling for going to school to become a licensed vocational nurse (LVN). I had to convince myself that I would still be in the medical profession.

We are all in this world with a purpose—an assignment—to complete. The vocation is ours. I really believed that my vocation was to be a doctor, and for many years I hurt with disappointment over not being able to achieve that goal.

As I completed LVN nursing school at the hospital, I worked at an X-ray clinic developing films and filing records. Later, I worked as a data processing operator at a hospital until I completed enough hours to be allowed to work as a nursing assistant. I completed my training in nursing school and finally became a bedside licensed nurse.

I took my state board exam. To this day, I think that board exam was the hardest thing I've ever done in my entire life. I thought I had failed, and back then we had to wait for results in the mail. Two weeks felt like an eternity to me.

Finally, I received my license in the mail. It was the beginning of my second-best vocation. My license read: "Be it known that Diana Labrada, having given satisfactory evidence of fitness, and having fulfilled all other requirements prescribed by law, is licensed to practice as a Licensed Vocational Nurse in the state of Texas." What an honor that was for me.

Many years later, I gave life to a talent God gave me at a very young age. I decided I was going to be a holistic practitioner. I opened a wellness center based on aromatherapy principles, massage, meditation, sound therapy, and other modern and ancient alternative-care methods. I named it 325 Massage Studio. The number 3 represents the Holy Trinity, the number 2 represents two heads are better than one -for when one falls the other can help him up, and the number 5 represents the five major wounds on Jesus' body.

This was the chapter in my life that changed me entirely. I met an angel. She made me realize that, had I become a doctor, I would have never met her. She was a very young patient who had been diagnosed with late-stage cancer. God gave me the honor and privilege to walk her home in prayer. She visited me regularly for spiritual guidance, prayer, meditation, and palliative care as doctors told her there was no cure and she had only months to live.

One night at eleven o'clock she called me from her hospital bed. She was dying. "Please, Diana, come to the hospital. I just need to feel your hands and hear your beautiful words of comfort." I was so tired from a long productive day at work. I prayed with her over the phone and told her, I'll be there early in the morning to see you. My dear whispered, "No, It has to be tonight. I may not be here tomorrow." I empowered myself to get up. I invited my sister to accompany me to the hospital to comfort her. During the entire twenty-five-minute drive to the hospital, I feared that the security guard would not let us in because visiting hours were over.

As soon as we stepped foot inside the hospital, it was as if the security guard had been waiting for us. He guided us straight to my patient's hospital floor. Divine intervention, I call it.

That moment has marked my heart and soul so deeply. Now I understand why going to Baylor College of Medicine was not in God's plan for me—this was His plan: being my brothers' and sisters' keeper, comforting those who are weak in spirit at their time of death or as they navigate difficult paths in life is truly my vocation.

Do not be tormented over situations that do not go your way. Being a doctor was my own plan, but God's plan was greater.

LIFE: A GRAND AIRPORT WHERE SOME PLANES ARRIVE AND OTHERS DEPART—ON TIME

An eleven-month-old baby at one breast and a newborn at the other—I still recall memories of my super-mom days. I burped the newborn baby while attempting to gently hold the other child with my leg to keep him from falling off the bed. It was quite a chore. He was hyperactive and strong. I became quite the expert at diaper changing. I could hold the eleven-month-old still for four seconds by entertaining him with a Barney plush toy while I, at great mega speed, changed the newborn child. This was my norm at just nineteen years old. How I managed nursing school, a job, an abusive partner, and motherhood is truly beyond my comprehension.

Life seemed so fast for me. It was as if life was a grand airport where some planes arrived and others departed. My children grew up way too fast. Time wasn't waiting for me; I compared it to the plane that departed on time. I was so busy working, going to school, and finding my own identity, that I missed many milestones in the lives of my children. In the blink of an eye, the plane had departed (on time). Just like that they grew up. I confess, I did what I could with what I had at the time; only this has kept me from feeling regret.

I thank God, for He has given me a second chance—my grandchildren. I am there for all occasions, and I love to build crazy memories with them, like spa day (the old-fashion kind—outside with the water hose). Although, my grandchildren think I am weird when I ask them to join me in my grounding and meditation sessions, I know they love me. We hug trees and embrace sunbathing and moon bathing every chance we get. Quality time is so important. In fact, we make up reasons to celebrate and be together often.

Keep your priorities straight: God first, then you, then family, and then everyone or everything else. We have no time to spare. We all have a destiny to fulfill. Don't miss your flight!

Do not live with regret. It is never too late to right your wrongs. Trust me—God conspires on our behalf. You always get a second chance.

KEYNOTE 4

DO NOT MISS YOUR MOMENT TO LAUGH AND DANCE LIKE THE LADY WHO WEPT IN DANCE SEASON

"A time to weep, and a time to laugh; a time to mourn, and a time to dance;" (Ecclesiastes 3:4 KJV).

In my twenty-nine-year career as a nurse and massage therapist, I have treated people of all walks of life. I have worked in hospital and clinic settings, and I have even taken work trips all over the world. One thing many of the people I met or patients I treated had in common, was that they wept in their season of laughter and dance.

I'll give you the example of a lady I treated just about every week for several years, during which time she continually believed that something bad was going to happen. She allowed fear and anxiety to overcome her thoughts, violating every spiritual law. In her human mind, she continually played the impending doom, and in due time, she impressed her subconscious with that belief.

In every session, I urged her to cancel her negative thoughts and look at all that was positive—all the good fruits in her life. She had beautiful and smart children, a loving husband, good cars, a nice home, a great job, and excellent health. I looked for many ways to direct her thoughts to "living in the now"—living in the season at hand. She regularly sought medical attention for anxiety and depression only to describe to me the feeling of stupor caused by the heavy medication she had been prescribed. Her feeling of impending doom worsened. She spoke of negativity but reached for tranquility through relaxation and the positivism I confessed in the sessions, often claiming that I brought her "back to earth."

After a few years, all the doom that she had been confessing took form when her husband contracted an incurable disease and, shortly afterwards, passed away. This now was her time to weep, only she had been weeping in her season of dance for many years. After her husband passed away, I never saw her in my office again.

Although I never did quite figure out what caused her to be so negative—perhaps an unfulfilled emotion within her or the spirit of negativity—to this day, I continue to bless her in secret and declare many days of laughter and dance for her.

THE DAILY REMINDERS THAT THE CREATOR CONSPIRES ON OUR BEHALF

I am very careful to speak defeat or lack in my life. However, I wasn't always this way. And, boy oh boy, did I ever see days of struggle in my life—days when all I had to offer was a piece of lint in my pocket. I had to remind myself that there was a kingdom where my riches lived.

One day, I drove down to the bank with only a few dollars to my name, hoping to make it in before my checks bounced. As doubt began to overpower my thoughts, I immediately felt an alluring sensation that led me to look down at a bush near the place where I had parked. What's that I see? A hundred-dollar bill—old and weathered by water, wind, and other struggles it had encountered.

It was as if it had been there forever. As I stared at it, I could only imagine the rough times it had gone through as it waited for my arrival.

Lucky, most might say, but for me it represented more. The area around the bank was beautifully landscaped with well-kept bushes, nicely trimmed, and recently trimmed at that. Now, can you explain why the yard guy did not see the hundred-dollar bill in all its magnificence? It was a message from God, perfectly revealed to my eyes. Had I not been sensitive to the feeling, I may very well have missed the blessing too. How many people had parked in that very spot for weeks, months, perhaps even years, and had not seen the money? But there it was—clearly with my name on it. I firmly believe that life is a quest in which we encounter struggles. But it is in the way we adapt and overcome adversity that we reveal blessings along the way.

I've learned to call my struggles "my period of training." Live with expectation of impending greatness by divine right. Quiet your spirit just a little, and you too will encounter hundred-dollar miracles. Be sensitive to Him, and quiet your spirit even more. Maybe larger miracles will be uncovered.

Here is another example: While planning a trip to Salt Lake City, Utah, to attend an essential oil convention, a deep thought came upon me. My 1998 Nissan Pathfinder had been leaving me stranded at every stop sign, but I had not fully pondered the thought that a new car was in my future until that day. *I want a BMW,* I thought to myself. In fact, the thought was so vivid it seemed it was a proclamation.

My friend and I completed our stay in Salt Lake City, and on our way back, her father decided to take us on a detour to Sun Ray Casino in Farmington, New Mexico. I walked into that casino empowered with expectation and positivism. We signed in at the counter and were awarded a five-dollar player bonus card. After playing the first machine, I won several hundred dollars. I then moved to the next machine and won several thousand dollars! As I continued playing, I felt a force leading me to a specific slot machine, which had a fishing theme. The corner of my eye kept wandering to it, but I ignored the feeling, telling myself, *Why would you move now if this machine is giving you winnings?* Finally, after this feeling persisted, I decided to move to the "fishing machine." It was sitting there empty and brightly shining with lights and adorned with fish and fishing rods. After a few spins—well, you wouldn't guess—I hit a $6,971 jackpot! There it was—my BMW.

When I arrived home, I went immediately to the dealership and paid the down payment for my BMW, a car I had given birth to first in thought. Even the color was perfect. It was a beautiful shade of green—Tasman Green to be exact. When I arrived home with my blessing, my sister yelled out, "Hey! It's Tasman Green—a gift from God!" It truly was just that—a gift—all because I'd had a thought and a vision and had believed in His promises.

OF ALL THE COLORS TO BE, BE GOLDEN

Colors in the Bible symbolize God and His majestic works. The Bible teaches us that God is the light. He is vibrant and captivating. It is important to dress in bright colors—colors that are spirited and vivacious. Natural, earthy tones are also energetic because they attract light.

Black, on the other hand, absorbs all the light, and extinguishes it. Satan exists in darkness. Black often symbolizes suffering, death, and mourning. This color is worn at funerals. You often see this color also worn for its slimming effect in formal evening wear and attire worn to glamorous events such as operas. But it is important to remember to contrast it with other colors, such as vibrant white, that attract light.

Red represents blood. We know from the Bible that, over 2,000 years ago, Christ died on the cross. He was the sacrificial lamb of God, and His blood is our redemption. Red is a color of incarnation, sacrifice, and vindication. It represents unconditional love and transcendent agape love.

Purple represents spiritual wealth, spirituality, nobility, and royalty. Purple symbolizes the sovereignty of Jesus Christ. It is a color of remembrance, sacredness, and the passion of Christ. Purple is the color of penitence when it is used during lent, a religious period of fasting, prayer, and almsgiving.

White represents purity and peace. The Holy Spirit is represented by a white dove. White is the color of light and the righteousness of Christ. As sinners, we are taught to come to Him and be made pure and white through His forgiveness. His mercy and grace make us clean again. White is the color of eternal peace and the color of the pearly gates of heaven.

Green represents prosperity. It represents a gift from God. It represents new beginnings—a rebirth. It is the color of life. Green is found in nature, so flourishing and alive. It symbolizes hope and tranquility. In the life of a Christian, it represents good fruit. It is the color of abundance and renewal.

In ancient times, people in higher ranks were adorned with gold. Kings, pharaohs, and noblemen alike celebrated with this illuminating color. Gold is one of the most precious metals. Gold was used to give homage and was one of the gifts brought to the newborn king—Jesus.

The Bible teaches us to be Christlike. Paul, in the book of Ephesians calls us to be "imitators of God" (Ephesians 5:1 NKJV). Gold represents God in all His richness and glory. Gold is guiding, much like the streets of gold that await us in God's Kingdom in Heaven. So, of all colors to be, choose to be golden.

Keynote 7

Do not Speak Lack or Want

"The Lord is my Shepherd; I shall not want." (Psalm 23:1 KJV).

In life, we should learn to neutralize thoughts of lack or want in all aspects. Take note of what you feel is lacking and remind yourself, *I shall not want peace, love, money or anything that may not be in this realm yet.* In Christ, we should have it *all*.

Here is a perfect example: On a day when you have no money in your pocket, do not declare, "I have no money." Instead say, "I shall not want money (I have it in Christ)." You may not see it now; it may not be in your realm yet. But start declaring your promises. Be bold! Claim your divine-right inheritance. The money will come. The peace, the love—whatever you feel you lack, you must lack no more, want no more. Declare, "I am rich in good fruits. I want not, I lack not."

Deeply root this belief in your mind. I call it my "riches affirmation." Once you declare this in your spirit, without a doubt, you will never experience lack or want in life knowing God is your Shepherd and that, through Him, you have it all.

If I am ever having a bad day, my mind is trained to think, *It is a sure indication that a blessing is on its way.*

KEYNOTE 8

THERE IS NO SUCH THING AS COMPETITION

Daily evaluation of character and a positive mindset will always keep you on track. In life, you should always remind yourself that, in the Divine Realm, there is no such thing as competition. I believe that God has a plan for *all* of us to prosper. To each He gives his or her own. There is no need to be lost in envy and rivalry.

In my practice, it is easy to get lost in worry, believing that other therapists might take my clients or students. Here is an example that makes the picture of my experience clearer. There was a company that was similar to mine across the street and two blocks down. In fact, there was one just about every fifteen miles, and all of them were open for business. I could easily have been discouraged and said, "There are too many to compete with. Why bother?" But instead, I proclaimed, "I am established, equipped, and empowered! I am a one-of-a-kind masterpiece, just as God says I am." This mindset proved successful. I went from eight faithful clients, to over a thousand! The floodgates of God's promise for prosperity opened up for me. This hunch—or as I call it "God's whisper"—pushed me to get started with just $10 to my name. Mine is a flourishing establishment, all because I never permitted my spirit to be attacked by the unease of competition and the fear of loss. I have learned to harness my emotions, and now I go from one blessing to another. I firmly believe in His plan for my prosperity, and my fountain never runs dry. Start giving your dreams direction; speak words of completion not competition.

Even before I ever started my business, I told people about my prosperous business. I wasn't lying because it was in my vision, and my word gave birth to that very vision. I remember a pastor who always used the phrase "Fake it till you make it!" We should remember that our highest good may still be in an invisible realm. Believe that all things are possible through Him. Hard work, dedication, and the right mindset will have you reach your highest good in no time. The business books will tell you that it takes two to four years to establish a successful business, but God can thrust you forward in no time. Trust in His biblical promises. Your appointed time is now: *One, two, three—start!*

KEYNOTE 9

BLESS AND BE BLESSED

I clearly remember a generous woman. She was a lady who loved to give to charities, causes, and events. Now, there is nothing wrong with that. In fact, God's law encourages alms-giving. This friend, however, was a "spotlight-seeker." She gave with a price— publicity. There she was posing for pictures that would appear on social media and in local newspapers and magazines as she handed over a plate of food or a box of new toys.

When doing God's work, we need to stay focused on doing it for His glory and not ours. Always do things as if unto God, for that which is done in secret will truly be rewarded. Don't get me wrong; giving to others is spiritually fulfilling, and we should encourage others to do the same. But before snapping that picture, we must acknowledge the purpose of the image. Is it to encourage others to give to a cause? Or, is it for our own glorification?

We need to also learn to give of our very best. Abraham, in his old age, was ready and willing to give his most precious gift—his son—as a sacrifice to show his love of God. What is our best offering? Is it our best or is it our scraps? I often pass by donation sites, and I can't help but notice some of the piles of trash that have been "donated." We must learn to give our best—the new dress hanging in our closet, our favorite shirt, that expensive perfume bottle. Often, we are quick to give up what we don't really like, what we no longer have use for, or what is worn and torn. From time to time, we need to sacrifice and give our very best too. We can trust that this will not go unnoticed.

> Each of you should give what you have decided in your heart to give, not reluctantly or under compulsion, for God loves a cheerful giver. God is able to bless you abundantly, so that in all things at all times, having all that you need, you will abound in every good work. (2 Corinthians 9:7–8 NIV)

HEALTH-THE GREATEST OF ALL FRUITS

Ralph Waldo Emerson wrote, "The first wealth is health."

This is one of the most exceptional and influential quotes I have ever come across. In my daily spiritual teachings, I strongly encourage my students, clients, friends, and family members to first place a conscious impression on what they think is most important; that is, what they consider true wealth.

Often, I ask my students to tell me their greatest desire or need. Most respond money or capital. That is not surprising in this economically fast-paced world, which makes it easy to place our conscious attention on the desire for money.

We must wholeheartedly understand that ideal health is the greatest fruit He will ever bestow: a sound mind, mental clarity, strong self-expression, physical endurance, and strong will power. A wholesome balance among body, mind, and spirit is indeed the principle wealth. Without health, even all the money in the world will be a disappointment. Every aspect of health empowers you to create the wealth and enables you to enjoy the fruits of your labor.

Most ill people I have treated declare, with great affirmation, ownership of disease, saying "my diabetes," "my psoriasis," "my "fibromyalgia" If they desire to be totally restored to health, they should stop claiming the diseases as theirs, and instead, declare themselves blessed with a resilient body that has the perfect ability and reflexes to heal itself. They should call upon vitality, vigor, self-expression, love, mental clarity, physical endurance, supernatural healing—all things given only by God.

We must remember that God has plans to prosper us and not to harm us. We need to ask Him for forgiveness from our incredulous ways of claiming disease. Do not let doubt cloud your thought, no matter how bad the prognosis is.

I have never forgotten a weak period in my life in which I declared "my" symptoms as my own demise. My friend scolded me. She immediately canceled my ownership of impending disease and proclaimed complete healing over every cell of my body, stopping me on this path to destruction. She shared with me a Bible verse that, to this day, I live by: "For God hath not given us the spirit of fear; but of power, and of love, and of a sound mind" (2 Timothy 1:7 NKJV).

Declare your fruits and thank God daily for your supernatural healing. Do not speak to your problem or illness. Instead, speak of the way out—the solution. Victory is yours in healing or any other petition through God's promise.

KEYNOTE 11

MELT AWAY STRESS AND CREATE PRECIOUS MOMENTS

Extensive scientific studies and clinical evaluations have proven that people live longer when they worry less. In my own personal observations, I have learned that, if you flood the brain with enough "feel-good sensations," an explosion of powerful chemical reactions occurs. Physiologically, an amazing reaction occurs in which hormone biochemicals are released with positive consequences. What exactly are these healing and powerful hormones, you ask? Endorphins and enkephalins are both responsible for healing and causing a sense of euphoria, or simply put, a sense of well-being. And who couldn't use a little of that!

As I compare progress notes of clients who let things go, prayed more, smiled or laughed at every chance, I find one similarity.

These clients had fewer occurrences of stress-triggered tiredness and pain than "champion worriers" experienced. People who pray and laugh almost always live longer, more effective, and more productive lives. In my clinical judgment, based on my daily client assessments and observations, most adrenal glitches that lab tests detect could have been avoided by a simple smile, giggle or laugh.

Start your healing journey by setting a time for daily quiet contemplation. During this time, explore effective strategies that can help you detour from the notorious, nagging thoughts of defeat! Learn to silence self-criticism and move past your slip-ups and confusion by letting things go. Find enjoyment in simple joys. Let go of all regret and melt away stress and burden! Giggle, smile, and laugh daily—even a fake laugh can lead to a real one. (Fake it till you make it!) Create precious moments by activating positive, feel-good reactions in your brain. Let the healing and well-being begin!

YOUR BRAIN WILL ALWAYS DISPLAY SIGNS AND SYMPTOMS TO ALERT YOU OF AN UNMET NEED

Do you ever find your head spinning as recurring thoughts whirl around? The ones you wish you could just press the clear button and automatically erase. These very thoughts are simply suppressed emotions and needs left unmet. Until you put an end to the unfulfilled thoughts, you will be a slave to the past. And the past may very well haunt you for a very long time, causing your subconsciousness to rehash thoughts. All of this places a heavy burden on your mental health.

Many of the negative emotions from which I have helped others heal happened to be broken love relationships. This reflects the need to feel loved and cherished as a woman or a man. Perhaps a parent, or a dear friend wronged you. These unmet emotions keep replaying in your mind as voids that arise from a need for feeling wanted, accepted, appreciated, or respected. Simply—this is the unmet need for unconditional love.

Keep a journal to express what you feel. Write down your most honest and intimate thoughts! This can give you a sense of release, and it may help you identify your need. Find ways to harness your emotions, whether it be by talking, writing, or praying about them. Let them go!

Neutralize the potency of negativity and pave your way to a life of peace and self-expression. Analyze the situation, identify the problem, and try to come up with a solution. The solution will bring you clarity and learning and will neutralize the past, making it an impotent state.

People can share with others only what they themselves possess. It is a vital lesson to master, especially when it comes to relationships.

I give you my own chapter that involved a very toxic love relationship, which existed at two very distant extremes. This man made me feel loved on some days, but on other days, he ignored my existence and fled the planet. I held onto a mythical idea, a fairy-tale love affair that, in all reality, never existed. Every last string of hope created false expectations for me, and a false image of who he really was. *He'll come around and want to marry me*, I told myself. In my mind, I wore the ring. During many nights, I justified the fact that he had not called me by deciding that he was healing. But the real truth was that he was with other women. In my disillusioned heart and mind, I was in the perfect "love story." I had buried myself in lies and falsehoods and was in desperate need to find a way out. I must admit the man never promised me a rose garden.

It wasn't until I stopped and identified my value—and, more importantly, my unmet needs—that I was able to pave my way to happiness. I needed to be loved unconditionally, not just when he felt like it. This was my reflection, my realization, and my solution. He was unable to give me what he did not have. He lacked luster with his poor self-respect, and selfishness. My spirit struggled with false ideas and hopes about a man who did not even love himself, much less have the capacity to offer anyone else unconditional love. The minute I understood this, my spirit healed.

In life, we need to realize that we cannot expect fruit from a barren desert. Now my spirit celebrates as it has reached mastery and sends him all the love, light, and good fruits from above.

Keynote 13

Living With Regret Leads to Illness and an Unfulfilled Destiny

It is very easy for our minds to travel in retrospect, but even easier to stay stuck in the past. When this happens, distant and tormenting memories cause short circuits and switch your brain from positivism and calm to the dangerous area of resentment and regret. Living in the past is a sure path to destruction. No doubt.

In fact, negative feelings brought upon by guilt and dark thoughts cause the body to produce degenerating acids. This chemical reactions will, in time, cause disease; for example, fibrosis, poor circulation, and autoimmune disease. These are just a few of the diseases that can be linked to the destructive results of unmet emotions. It is vital to use the past as learning experiences, but not as roadblocks or sinkholes.

Surround yourself with people who stimulate positive biochemicals. Most importantly, stay away from people who enable your dysfunction—the dream crushers, the fault-finders, and especially the history keepers who keep account of your every sin and wrong with great detail.

One must be cautious not to suppress negative feelings with sedatives or stimulants because such a fix is only temporary. Moreover, these things can actually keep you chained to lack and limitation, which keep you from your destiny.

Take the story of a man I knew who was a functional alcoholic. He performed duties at work with prestige and great diligence, but as soon as he clocked out, alcohol became his "escape." Or so he thought. Unfortunately, all the alcohol did was trigger resentment and ill feelings, which kept him from healing. He was unable to move forward from the past.

Cherish lived moments, but don't let them torment you or keep you stagnant. Speak to your torment with firmness! Say, "I have no room for delay. Defeat and regret, move out of my way! I have precious moments to create and a destiny to fulfill!"

FEAR IS ONLY AN ILLUSION-REACH MASTERY OF NO LIMITATIONS

"For God hath not given us a spirit of fear, but of power, and of love, and of a sound mind (2 Timothy 1:7 NKJV)

The Bible teaches us that we are not to worry or fear. Yet, many of us live lives that feed fear. We do this with more regularity than we do feeding trust, courage, calmness, and equanimity. Worry is not just an emotional hazard. It has physical and spiritual implications. It reveals itself as disease or disequilibrium against a sound body, mind, and spirit—your wholeness. Perturbation will dry out your bones and will make you progressively sick. Take for example our brother Job- (Job3:25) scripture teaches us that the very things he feared came upon him.

Most of the future matters we worry about, as it turns out, never even happen how we imagined. All these matters of distress and gloom, many come to realize, are only illusions or negative creations of our own imaginations. Thoughts impress the subconscious. They take hold and manifest as fruits, but unfortunately, also as plagues. I've learned to trust that things just work themselves out, and I do not entertain worry or fear.

People who have never walked your path will never understand your journey. Live to make yourself happy. Do not worry about what others think of you. Trust that God has redeemed you.

2 Timothy 1:7 tells us that God did not give us a spirit of fear. It clearly states that we were given power, love, and a sound mind.

When we deeply root these gifts in our spirit and believe beyond a shadow of a doubt that God has equipped us with a fearless spirit of power, love, and sound mind, it is then that we reach a mastery of no limitations. Fear, worry and limitations do not exist, except if we accept them in our minds. Constant positive affirmations and unwavering faith are the only tools necessary for retaining the gifts. Use your spirit of power, love, and sound mind to impress positivism into your conscious and subconscious mind. Empower your intellectual capabilities, heal and live a life of great abundance and life-changing wisdom of spiritual law.

KEYNOTE 15

GUARD YOUR HEART AGAINST GREED

Be intentional on guarding your heart against greed. Remember that generosity will destroy greed. Every garden tells its own story. What story do you want to tell? Do not allow greed to grab hold of you. Tell the story about why you have been blessed and how you gave to receive. Let the abundant blessings of God define your story.

Think about the parable in Luke 12: Jesus reminds us not to be afraid; instead, we should reflect on the foolishness of becoming too attached to wealth. Once we can master that our riches and blessings are in heaven, generosity follows.

Greed has got to be one of the worst self-destructive acids. Greedy people are often self-centered; they lack empathy and are really never satisfied. Most of them are experts at manipulation and display a strong desire for the possessions of others. They almost always focus on satiating their own selfish desires. These people are the masters of loopholes and will find every way to outsmart the system.

Greedy people can be very dangerous. They have allowed greed to overtake their principles. Take, for example, the Bible story in Genesis of Cain and Abel. Cain killed Abel because God blessed Abel. God accepted Abel's offering over Cain's. Cain's obvious motive was greed and jealousy.

Stay away from greedy people. God will not bless people who have corrupt minds until they remove greed from their hearts. Greedy people will never rejoice for your accomplishments or blessings. They are blinded with scales of envy and their own failed situations. The greatest danger with greedy people is that they cannot be happy for you because it exposes their own weaknesses. Whatever your blessing is, they hate that they do not have it. They are blind to the simple principle: One must first give to receive. They lack temperance and generosity. In their ill minds, greed is easier than edification of the accomplishments or great achievements of others.

Greedy people cause you to doubt yourself. They are those who will tell you: "You're not enough." "You're going to fail." "Gas is too high." "This is the worst time to start." "That's a dumb idea." "You need a higher degree." "There is too many in the market." The list goes on.

If someone acts against you or your plans, do not attack in return. Remove yourself from situations that cause you evil thoughts or cause you to doubt yourself. Continue to bless greedy people by praying for them and wishing them their highest good.

In life, people will go up against you. Greed will attack. Do not be shaken or allow greed to be a barricade that keeps you from the blessings God has for you.

I have treated many people who have been governed by fast-paced lives directed by envy. Many of them carried pent-up emotions from many years of unresolved conflicts, anger, jealousy, and excessive envy. When dealing with difficult situations like that, I first try to identify the defense that drove them towards excess.

Oftentimes, it was the drive that came from the idea that the more they made, the more they wanted. It is especially tough in a society like ours.

As my brothers' and sisters' keeper, I always try to introduce the essential principles in life: unconditional love, self-love, and self-acceptance.

I often express the biblical principle of giving and receiving. We must understand that, in order to receive, we must learn to give, and that God can bless you only if you rid your heart of envy and greed.

Dealing with greedy people is never easy. It requires much persistence, love, humility, and commitment. Some will become greedier, and others will move on to a simple happy life. In my book, a happy life is a rich life.

Affirmations for every day of the week

SUNDAY

Day 1: I shall not live in fear. Fear is not of God.

Monday

Day 2: I stand with confidence for God has given me power, love, and a sound mind.

TUESDAY

Day 3: Negative thoughts of fear and limitations do not exist and cannot enter my mind unless I let them.

WEDNESDAY

Day 4: Today I will live my life with purpose. I will fulfill my destiny.

THURSDAY

Day 5: I will celebrate life with gratitude. All my provision comes from above.

FRIDAY

Day 6: Life is a Journey of great adventure with God in it.

SATURDAY

Day 7: I now live with assurance and expectation of the great Promises God has for me.

CPSIA information can be obtained
at www.ICGtesting.com
Printed in the USA
BVHW071334160621
609638BV00005B/358